INFORMATION EXPLORER JUNIOR

Post It!
Sharing Photos with Friends and Family

by Suzy Rabbat

CHERRY LAKE PUBLISHING · ANN ARBOR, MICHIGAN

A NOTE TO PARENTS AND TEACHERS: Please remind your children how to stay safe online before they do the activities in this book.

CHERRY LAKE
Publishing

A NOTE TO KIDS: Always remember your safety comes first!

Published in the United States of America
by Cherry Lake Publishing
Ann Arbor, Michigan
www.cherrylakepublishing.com

Content Adviser: Gail Dickinson, PhD, Associate Professor, Old Dominion University, Norfolk, Virginia

Photo Credits: Cover, ©Lisa F. Young/Dreamstime.com; page 5, ©neelsky/ Shutterstock, Inc.; page 6, ©Xi Zhang/Dreamstime.com; page 7, ©jokerpro/ Shutterstock, Inc.; page 8, ©wavebreakmedia ltd/Shutterstock, Inc.; page 12, ©Monkey Business Images/Shutterstock, Inc.; page 13, ©Feng Yu/Shutterstock, Inc.; page 14, ©iStockphoto.com/william87; page 15, ©vectorlib-com/Shutterstock, Inc.; page 21, ©Jaimie Duplass/Shutterstock, Inc.

Library of Congress Cataloging-in-Publication Data
Rabbat, Suzy.
  Post it! : sharing photos with friends and family/ by Suzy Rabbat.
    p. cm. — (Information explorer junior)
  Audience: For grades K to 3.
  Includes bibliographical references and index.
  ISBN 978-1-61080-485-1 (lib. bdg.) — ISBN 978-1-61080-572-8 (e-book) —
ISBN 978-1-61080-659-6 (pbk.)
1. Photography—Digital techniques—Juvenile literature. 2. Image files—Juvenile literature. 3. Computer file sharing—Juvenile literature. I. Title.
  TR267.R326 2013
  770.285—dc23   2012009706

Cherry Lake Publishing would like to acknowledge the work of The Partnership for 21st Century Skills. Please visit www.21stcenturyskills.org for more information.

Printed in the United States of America
Corporate Graphics Inc.
July 2012
CLFA11

Table of Contents

CHAPTER ONE

Know Your Camera

Point and zoom! Click and print! It's fun and easy to take **digital** photos! This diagram shows the basic parts of a digital camera.

- Power Button — Press to turn your camera on and off.
- Shutter Button — Press this button all the way down to take your picture.

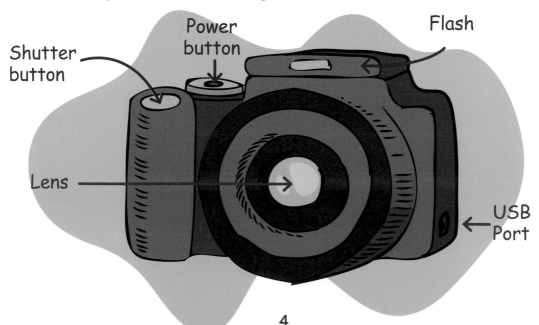

Shutter
button

Power
button

Flash

Lens

USB
Port

In addition to still shots, some digital camera also record video clips.

- Display Panel — This is a window on the back of your digital camera. It shows what your camera sees.
- USB Port — Use this port to plug in a cable. This cable connects your camera to your computer.
- Lens — This is the camera's eye. It sees whatever you point it at.
- Zoom Button — This lets you **focus** the lens on objects that are far away or close by.

Holding your camera with two hands will help you focus your picture.

How to Hold Your Camera

Most digital cameras are small. You can hold them in one hand. But you can take better photos if you use both hands to hold the camera. It's as easy as 1-2-3!

1. Use your thumbs and index fingers to hold the bottom and top of the camera.
2. Wrap your other fingers around the sides of the camera.
3. Keep one index finger free to press buttons.

Hold your camera steady when you press the shutter button. Keep your elbows close to your sides. Try not to move around. Your pictures may come out blurry if you move too much.

Keep your fingers away from the lens. They can get in the way of your photo!

Take a deep breath and hold it before you snap your photo. This will help you keep your camera steady.

CHAPTER TWO

Photo-Taking Tips

It's easy to practice your photography skills with a digital camera. You can take a lot of shots. Delete the ones you don't like. Try these helpful tips as you practice.

Practice taking photos from a variety of angles. How is each photo different?

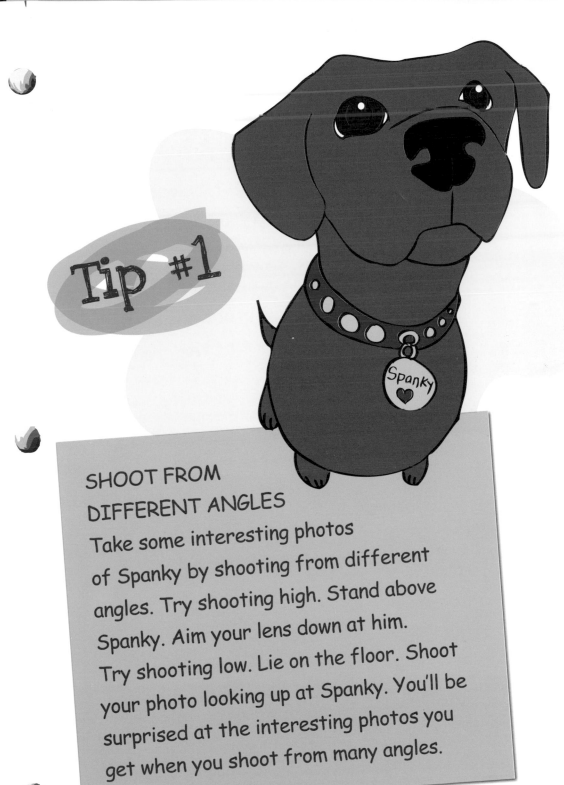

Tip #1

SHOOT FROM DIFFERENT ANGLES

Take some interesting photos of Spanky by shooting from different angles. Try shooting high. Stand above Spanky. Aim your lens down at him. Try shooting low. Lie on the floor. Shoot your photo looking up at Spanky. You'll be surprised at the interesting photos you get when you shoot from many angles.

Tip #2

GET CLOSE OR ZOOM OUT

Zooming in is one way to get a close-up shot. Close-ups can help you show a lot of details in your photo. You can also get closer to your subject by taking a few steps toward it. Zoom out or move backward to capture more of the area around your subject.

You can zoom in on your subject to show smaller details.

KEEP IT STRAIGHT

Look at the image in the display window before you press the shutter button. Is it tilted to one side? Move one side of the camera higher or lower to straighten out the image.

Tip #3

To get a copy of this activity, visit www.cherrylakepublishing.com/activities.

Activity

Decide on a subject to photograph. Your subject could be a friend or a pet. Take several practice shots. Use high and low angles. Practice zooming in and out. Then look at all the photos you took. Which ones are most interesting? Are the photos focused and straight? You're on your way to taking awesome photos!

CHAPTER THREE

Other Tools for Taking Pictures

Many **mobile devices** have built-in cameras. Most new cell phones and computers can be used to take pictures.

Cell phone cameras make it east to take photos anywhere.

12

Scanners let you make digital versions of pictures you draw in paper.

A camera that's connected to your laptop makes it easy to take photos of yourself!

A **document scanner** can also create digital images. Do you like to draw? You can create digital images of your drawings by scanning them. Document scanners take pictures of documents. Then they load the pictures onto your computer. Try scanning your artwork. You can e-mail the scanned image to Grandma. You can also use it to create a birthday card for Uncle Joe.

To get a copy of this activity, visit www.cherrylakepublishing.com/activities.

Activity

E-mail isn't the only way to share digital images with friends and family members. Many people like to create online photo albums. Flickr, Webshots, and Picasa are among the most popular Web sites for creating photo albums. Ask an adult to set up an account and help you upload some of your scanned drawings or digital photos. Now all of your friends can see your creations!

Online photo sharing sites are easy and fun.

CHAPTER FOUR

Photo Projects to Share

There are many ways to share your digital images with others. Let's look at some project ideas.

Zoos are great places to take interesting photos.

To get a copy of this activity, visit www.cherrylakepublishing.com/activities.

Activity

PHOTO JOURNAL

Are you planning to visit the zoo soon? Be sure to take plenty of photos to remember the event. You can keep track of your photos in a small notebook. Make notes to help you remember important ideas each time you take a picture. Name the animals you saw at the zoo. Write down an interesting fact you learned about each one.

Are you creating a photo journal about your family vacation? Write in your notebook the date you took each photo. Also write where you were and what you did.

PHOTO JOURNAL

You can print the photos and paste them into a **scrapbook** after you return from your trip. Write a sentence or two below each photo. Use the notes in your notebook to tell an interesting story. Your scrapbook will help you remember your vacation for many years!

Many photo Web sites allow you to print scrapbooks using the photos you have posted online.

To get a copy of this activity, visit www.cherrylakepublishing.com/activities.

Activity

GREETING CARDS

Want to send a special birthday wish to a friend or relative?

1. Start by taking a photo of yourself. You can use the camera on your laptop computer. You can also ask someone to take your picture with a digital camera. Save the photo to your computer desktop.

2. Now open a word processing program. Such programs include Microsoft Word and Pages for Mac.

3. Start with a blank document. Ask an adult to help you adjust the page setup to "landscape."

4. Drag your image onto your blank document. Or copy the image and paste it in the document. You may have to make the image smaller. Start by clicking on the image. Then click on a corner and drag it toward the middle of the image.

5. Slide your image to the bottom right corner of the document.
6. Print the page.
7. Line up the short edges of the page. Fold the paper in half and crease the left side. Keep your photo on the outside.
8. Fold the paper in half one more time. Keep the fold on the top.
9. Write your greeting on the outside of the card. Add your message on the inside. Now you have a homemade birthday card to send!

To get a copy of this activity, visit www.cherrylakepublishing.com/activities.

Activity

You can use digital images to make all kinds of cards and notes. You can make everything from party invitations to get well cards. Try making a fun thank-you card! Take a photo of yourself holding a gift someone gave you. Put the photo on the front of the card. Draw a speech bubble or make one with your word processing program. Then add the words "Thank you!" or "This is awesome!" in big letters!

Take time to think about your photography skills as you practice taking pictures. Do you shoot from many angles? Are your images clear and straight? Think of ways to improve your photos. Even the greatest photographers are always looking for ways to get better. Be creative and have fun as you share your images with friends and family!

What kinds of photos will you take next?

Glossary

digital (DIJ-i-tuhl) able to be read and displayed by
   a computer

document scanner (DAHK-yuh-muhnt SKAN-ur) a device
   that makes a digital image from paper or a printed photo

focus (FOH-kus) adjust the lens of a camera to see something
   clearly

mobile devices (MOH-buhl di-VISE-iz) small, handheld
   computers and cell phones

scrapbook (SKRAP-buk) a book with blank pages on
   which pictures, newspaper clippings, and other items
   can be mounted

Find Out More

BOOKS

Bidner, Jenni. *The Kids' Guide to Digital Photography: How to Shoot, Save, Play with, and Print Your Digital Photos*. New York: Sterling Publishing, 2011.

Rabbat, Suzy. *Using Digital Images*. Ann Arbor, MI: Cherry Lake Publishing, 2010.

WEB SITES

Kodak
www.kodak.com
Click in the search field and type in "fun for kids." You'll find lots of digital photo activities to do and share.

Photo Op
www.nga.gov/kids/zone/photoop.htm
This interactive Web site lets you practice your photography skills without a camera!

Shutterfly
www.shutterfly.com
Use your photos to make picture books, photo albums calendars and more.

Index

About the Author

Suzy Rabbat is a national board certified school librarian who works as a school library consultant. She lives in the northwest suburbs of Chicago.